know me,
hold me,
sing to me

what my grandchild
taught me about God

know me,
hold me,
sing to me

kathleen chesto

 SORIN BOOKS™   Notre Dame, Indiana

© 2004 by Kathleen O'Connell Chesto

All rights reserved. No part of this book may be used or reproduced in any manner whatsoever, except in the case of reprints in the context of reviews, without written permission from Sorin Books, P.O. Box 1006, Notre Dame, IN 46556-1006.

www.avemariapress.com

International Standard Book Number: 1-893732-70-3

Cover and text design by

Printed and bound in the United States of America.

Library of Congress Cataloging-in-Publication Data

Chesto, Kathleen O.
  Know me, hold me, sing to me : what my grandchild taught me about God
/ Kathleen O'Connell Chesto.
      p. cm.
  ISBN 1-893732-70-3 (pbk.)
  1. Grandparents—Religious life. 2. Grandparenting—
Religious aspects. I. Title.
BV4528.5 .C48 2004
248.8'45—dc22

                                                    2003021286

Acknowledgments

... to Tom McGrath, who suggested the book

... to Frank Cunningham, who edited and nurtured the book

... to John Kirvan, who focused the book

... to Betsy Demeyer, who read and critiqued the book

... to my family, who supported and loved the book

... to Katie, who inspired the book

Thanks.

Kathleen O'Connell Chesto

Sometimes, we don't choose our symbols for God.

Sometimes, they choose us.

S. Jorgensen

Contents

8

Introduction

In a beautiful children's book by Sandy Eisenberg Sasso, all the people that God created begin to search for God's name. The tired soldier names God "Peace," the lonely child names God "Friend," the farmer names God "Source of Life," and the woman nursing her infant names God "Mother." As more and more names are given to God, the people begin to argue with one another. Each one insists there can be only one name for God, and it is the one he or she has chosen. The story tells us, "No one listened. Not even God." Ultimately the people find their solution when they discover that each of them is a reflection of God.

A wise poet once observed there are some things about which nothing can be said, but before which we dare not remain silent. It is certainly true that there is nothing we can say about God, no name we can give, no symbol we can create, that scratches the surface of God's reality. To insist that our name encompasses God, that it is the only correct name—no matter how beautiful

9

or accurate it may be—makes an idol out of our symbol.

But to remain silent, to give God no name at all, denies us the possibility of entering into a personal relationship with God. So we dare not remain silent. Each of us needs a way to name God if we are to pray. And just like the people in Sasso's book, in some way, each of our names flows out of our own experience.

Sometimes those names are given to us in childhood, or perhaps fostered in a religious tradition, framed in the prayers the tradition taught us. Sometimes we discover those names as adults, as we study, search, or listen for God. And sometimes those names emerge from the very depths of our being, taking us by surprise.

Enter Katherine Emily

Nothing prepared me for the impact of becoming a grandparent. Parenting, with all its profound joy and deep pain, taught me who I am and who I am called to be. But grandparenting has given me a whole new image of God.

Katherine Emily is the daughter of our older daughter, our first grandchild. She was born on December 8, 2001, less than three months after the September terrorist attack. I was still paralyzed by a post-traumatic shock that made no sense, to me or to anyone else. I had not lost family, or close friends, or even income, in the attack. But I had lost my neighbor's children, my children's friends, my faith in my own significance, my belief, not in God, but in a God who cared, a God to whom any of us actually mattered.

Enter Katherine Emily.

It was a gray, dismal evening when our granddaughter arrived. The rain which had threatened all day had settled into a freezing drizzle, as if the world wept tears of ice. I was so unfamiliar with this whole grandparenting process, I had not even known we could go to the hospital, until my younger daughter insisted. She would be helping to deliver the baby. Of course, her Dad and I would want to be there to welcome this little one! "Of course, the hospital will let you!"

And so I stood at the window in the family lounge of the hospital, feeling useless and strange, my ears bombarded with the cacophony of the birthing suites. The cries of several newborns mixed with the sounds of our younger daughter's voice counting loudly from a nearby room where she coached her big sister through labor.

At 9:06, one distinct small cry made my heart jump in my chest, and I turned to the others in the room and announced, "She's here."

A wary skepticism greeted my quiet proclamation. "How could you know, with all this noise?"

"Somebody note the time. We'll check when Steve comes to tell us."

I did not need my son-in-law to confirm the time for us; my heart knew. At the sound of her voice, I had felt the universe shift, and tears had sprung unbidden to my eyes. I turned to the window to proclaim the great news to the dripping world beyond the pane, but the earth already knew. The rain had turned to snow, and the street lamps were sending sparkling paths across silvery white lawns.

I simply had not anticipated my knowing, my being so deeply moved. It had been a long and difficult pregnancy. The morning sickness had lingered throughout the days, then stretched to fill the entire nine months. I had held my daughter in my arms countless times as the nausea and vomiting left her tearfully committed to never having another child. Too many people had told her it would all be forgotten in the joy of the baby, but that just didn't matter in the pain of the moment.

As I stood quietly by the hospital window, I thought I knew what it felt like to be God, to watch your child suffer, to know that the only way out of the suffering would be to destroy the new life it heralds.

Sometimes we have to hold on in the pain and wait for the joy.

Moments later, as I held earth's newest child in my arms, the darkness of my own post 9/11 world cracked, and the God I was certain I had lost discovered me.

Grandparent God, is it you?

The Big Picture

Most of my spiritual life has been focused on trying to see "the big picture." So often, what I think the picture is, turns out to be only a thread in the tapestry. It is similar to those mosaic jigsaw puzzles in which each piece holds its own distinct little picture. Put them all together and the big picture turns out to be something totally different than expected. A close inspection of a finished puzzle that depicts a rocket blasting off reveals a thousand tiny pictures of completely separate realities. My life, at any moment, is one of those tiny pictures, constantly being incorporated into the bigger reality.

In my prayer, I have struggled for years to keep the big picture in mind, to tell myself I am weaving on the back of the tapestry and cannot see the final outcome. A hundred spiritual writers have mentored me in that vision. "Don't miss the forest for the trees" has been repeated so often in my life that I have come to believe its value, without ever questioning the message.

Until Katie.

My granddaughter, fifteen months old as I write this, enters a room and zeroes in immediately on the smallest, most insignificant object in it. It may be a piece of dead leaf dragged into the house on the dog's fur. It might be a tiny piece of macaroni that escaped the pot, or a bit of fluff from a deteriorating cushion. Her radar takes her directly to it. She picks it up carefully in her newly developed pincer grip, eyeing, admiring, moving it from one hand to the other, and eventually tasting. It will absorb her indefinitely if it does not fall apart or get taken away. Is it because it is out of place, or is it simply because it is the most insignificant piece in the whole picture?

I am always surprised by what she finds. It has invariably escaped my attention, almost as if it rested in a blind spot in my vision. Has my attention to the big picture been creating blind spots? I am suddenly reminded of castles where I have been so overwhelmed by the magnificence of the building that I failed to notice the intricate carving in the woodwork; or of redwood forests where the majesty of the trees blotted out the violets in the undergrowth.

Katie's awareness suggests to me that a God, whose big picture not only includes all of us but reaches beyond the created universe, might actually be focused on me.

Grandparent God, have I been missing the tree for the forest?

Homecoming

One of the strongest memories from my childhood has, at its heart, no important occasion, no life-altering decision. I am amazed that, as a ten-year-old, I would even recognize its significance, let alone remember it now.

It was a bitter cold December evening, one of the shortest days of the year and the recipient of the first good snowfall. My friend and I had spent the brief daylight time that remained after school sledding down the long, terraced hill near her home. Oblivious to the cold and the encroaching dark, we let the night catch us unprepared. We were both late for supper, very late. We ran the short distance to her house, then I headed up our deserted country road alone, dragging my sled, for the half-mile journey home.

Street lights were still in the distant future for this quiet country town, and the only illumination I could count on for this walk was from the seven homes I would pass on the way. But most of the families were already at supper in their kitchens in the back of their houses; only a faint glimmer of light actually drifted out to the street. The moonless, starry night, the spectral darkness that seemed to reflect off the snow, started to spook me. I began to worry that I had paid so little attention to the time, that my mother would be angry with me for being late for dinner. The eerie darkness began to invade my thoughts and dissipate the joy of the first good sledding of the season.

My own house came into view, its porch light piercing the darkness. The knot of tension in my stomach gently released. Inside, someone was waiting for me, the porch beacon said so. Inside it was warm, and supper would be filling the kitchen with good, savory smells. I stood absolutely still for a moment, holding the darkness and light in some sacred place inside me, admonishing myself that this moment was important and needed to be remembered somehow. Then I broke into a run, slipping across the snow and trudging through the drifts with the longing to be home.

I have experienced many homecomings since that night, homecomings from school, from college, from hospital stays, even from the home I created with my husband. There have been many meals waiting for me in that big country kitchen and lots of warm welcomes. But something about the porch light in the midst of the cold and the darkness all those years ago remains with me. Sometimes we really need the dark to understand the light that draws us home.

Waiting in the Light

I lay my granddaughter carefully in the crib in the bedroom. Her parents will be here soon, but sleep came as soon as darkness settled over the world outside our windows. I do not want to leave a light on and risk her awakening in a strange place and being frightened. I crack the door, allowing a splinter of light to creep through, knowing she will recognize it as proof that someone waits in the light for her.

> *Grandparent God, do you send splinters of light into my dark nights to remind me of your presence? Are they invitations to call out? Or reassurances to rest quietly in the darkness a little longer?*

Time

I am getting nothing done. As long as this baby is in the house, time stands still. When she is awake, I want to play with her, read to her, sing to her. When she is sleeping, I sit and watch her.

Grandparent God, do you gaze on me with the same delight that overpowers me in the presence of this little one? Do you "waste" whole days because you love me so much you can't take your eyes off of me?

Holy
Litter

My home is becoming an obstacle course. There is a high chair in the small dining room, a crib in the kitchen sporting the same mobile my granddaughter has at home. There are diapers and toys, bottles and bowls, baby tub and changing table, tripping us up at every turn. All so that my granddaughter will feel more at home in this place that is not her home, reminders of her own Mom and Dad, her own particular space in the universe, while she is away from it.

Do you litter my world, Grandparent God, with reminders of you, of my real home? Is it all to make me comfortable in the space I share for a little while? Indulgent grandparent that you are, I stumble across your love at every turn.

God of
Shadow

For my fiftieth birthday, my youngest presented me with a small box accompanied by a little story. She related that she had been walking to class one sunny morning, tired and depressed, oblivious to everything but her own feet. As she walked, she began to notice her shadow, elongated in the early morning light. It was slipping unobserved across the shoes of other pedestrians walking at a slower pace or in the opposite direction. She offered a startling insight: "I think our shadows are our angels, stretching out behind us, touching others without our even knowing." In the box was a carved little angel and the promise that she would remain as close to me as my shadow.

The angel still sits on my bureau reminding me of my daughter's inspiration. Our shadows are holy, a part of us capable of touching others without our realization. Much has been said about our shadow side, but none of it measures up to Liz's observation. "Our shadows are our angels. . . ."

Loving the Shadows

The light dancing off the leaves trickles through the windows making intricate patterns on the rough stone of the fireplace. Katie watches entranced by the delicate movement. She refuses to be distracted by voices, or toys, or various appeals for her attention. No light is as intriguing to her as this remnant of light denied. I hold her patiently, not wanting to disrupt her vigorous concentration. As I watch, I wonder if she, like Liz, is seeing angels dance.

When do we stop loving the shadows and start loving only the light?

Grandparent God, enchant me with the shadows as you once enchanted me with your light.

Colic

I was working late in my office and came upstairs to unexpectedly find my daughter working in the dining room. The infant seat was on the table, sharing space with the papers Becky had spread out as she completed an assignment for her master's degree program. Katie was sleeping soundly.

"Hi, Mom," my daughter whispered. "She just wouldn't go to sleep. She has been crying non-stop for the last two hours. I finally put her in the car and started driving randomly. I was going all over when it dawned on me to come here. I knew you or Dad would walk her and give me a break and maybe I could get some work done. By the time I got here, she was asleep. So I set up shop."

She finished with a rueful smile lighting up her tired eyes.

I am touched more deeply than I would have thought possible. I am honored that my daughter would trust me with her frustration and her need. I look lovingly at the tiny baby causing all this commotion and the exhaustion in my daughter's face. I can only hope our home will always be a place of refuge for them both.

Grandparent God, do you feel honored when I dump my needs on you, when I turn to you, again and again, frustrated and exhausted, beyond my own ability to cope? Hide me, then, in the shelter of your wings.

Being Known

My work takes me all over North America, and I seem to spend an inordinate amount of time with no real idea where I am going. I know the name of my contact, often the person who will meet me at the airport, perhaps to whisk me away to another city that might not have even been mentioned in our correspondence. I give many talks at convention centers, hotels, and places other than the home location of the group that did the inviting. The person meeting me has only my picture to go on. I have only my faith that someone will come and pick me up. Recently, I have started wondering if I shouldn't get a little more information before I start out, just in case.

On one recent trip, I walked down the jetway into a strange airport, knowing only that my final destination was about two hours away. As I stepped into the teeming crowd, I experienced a moment of real panic. I appeared to be the only one in thousands who did not know where she was going. I was not even all that sure where I was. My bag was with me, so I was deprived of the comfort of following the signs for baggage. And it looked as if no one was there for me.

I waited tentatively by security, trying to quiet my heart as I figured out my next move. I could always try paging. What *was* the name of the person who was supposed to meet me? If I couldn't find it, I could always page myself, and then they would know where *I* was. As I fumbled through my briefcase, I heard a voice.

"Dr. Chesto? Kathy Chesto?" In that moment, at the sound of that voice, I knew everything was all right. I did not actually know any more than I had known two seconds earlier. I did not even know the person who spoke. But someone knew *me*, and that was all that mattered. Someone had called me by name.

Called by Name

Katie is two months old. I was babysitting for her today. She had awakened from her nap and had been happily cooing to her Winnie the Pooh mobile for several minutes. As I approached her crib, she looked up into my eyes.

"Hi, Katie, love," I greeted her. At the sound of her name, her face broke into an explosive smile.

I am not sure if she knows me yet. But she knows her name. And she knows that *I* know *her,* and that is enough.

> *Grandparent God, even when I find it so hard to know you, help me remember that it is enough to know I am known. You have called me by name.*

Dark Night

Today, my daughter's maternity leave ended.

My granddaughter weeps inconsolably for her missing mother. It is not the distinct wail of hunger, the angry cry of discomfort, the petulant cry of boredom, all of which I have come to know. This is a cry of infinite sadness that swells her little eyes from the incessant tears. She will not take the bottle I offer. She wants her mother's breast. She will not nap, although exhaustion makes her body limp. I can do nothing but hold her in my arms and rock her with lullabies. She refuses to be comforted. She is oblivious to my love, and my own tears of frustration and pain fall on her face and blanket.

How can she feel so abandoned and alone when she is cradled in such love?

Do you hold me, Grandparent God, in those darkest moments, those moments when I feel abandoned and alone? Are you cradling me in your arms, whispering soothing lullabies I refuse to hear, offering nourishment I cannot bear to accept? Let me be content in knowing you are there. Help me to be content in being there for this heartbroken baby.

Presence

Madonna and child cuddle in the corner of my sofa. The early sunlight, allowed easy access to the windows by barren winter trees, rests on both their heads. A veil of long, curly dark hair hangs across the breast where the infant happily satisfies her morning hunger.

We are discussing the Baptism.

"I just want you to be there, Mom."

We are not talking about my physical presence. Of course I will be there.

"I would love Katie to be in your baptism tape, and Steve and I would not mind at all. But I don't want you doing the taping. I just want you to be there."

I am making videos on sacraments for Twenty-Third Publications. What a wonderful time to be doing a video on baptism, when your own grandchild is being baptized! I will get such wonderful close-ups of the pouring of the water, the anointing, the white garment and the candle. I will capture Steve and Becky's resolute look when the pastor asks them, "What do you ask of the church for this child?" I can see it all in my mind's eye, where all great videos take shape.

"It's okay if you need to do this, Mom. But I want you to understand how I feel. I just want you to be there."

Oh, I understand, and the truth of your plea echoes in a thousand other guilty chambers in my heart. You want me to be there, not as video producer, not as camera person, one step removed from the celebration by the lens through which I view it. You want me to be there as your mother, as Katherine Emily's grandmother. You want me to be there for no other reason but you.

Yes, I will be there.

> Grandparent God, I know you are there. I need to know you are there for me.

The Telephone

"How's Katie, Mom?"

It is my daughter, calling from work, worrying about her own daughter.

"Would you like to talk to her?"

I hold the receiver to my granddaughter's ear. A smile begins to form as she hears her mother's voice. She turns to look at the receiver, and her face crumples into a sad little cry. She cannot believe in the voice without the face. Without the familiar eyes to gaze into and the familiar, warm smell, the black piece in her grandmother's hand is a cruel hoax.

We will try again when she is older.

Grandparent God, do I reject your voice simply because I cannot see your face?

Eyes

I am going to break down and get bifocals. It's time. When I am speaking to a large group, I have to choose between seeing my audience or seeing my notes. My memory, or lack of it, no longer allows me to do talks without notes. But I have discovered that the ability to see into the eyes of my listeners is just as important to me as the notes, although I am only beginning to understand why.

When I finish speaking, I am always drained to the point where it is difficult to stand up or even speak. This is partly due to my multiple sclerosis, no doubt, but I have long suspected it is more than that. A dear friend once suggested to me that my weakness was like the gospel story where the woman with the hemorrhage touched Jesus' robe and he felt power go out from him. According to my friend, the people were touching my robe, draining me of power and strength.

Instinctively, I knew she was wrong, but her response still offered the insight I needed. It is not my robe being touched. I am the woman doing the touching, and the people are Jesus, who wear the robe. The power I experience comes from them.

But the touch is not a physical one. We commune with our eyes, and it is the strength, the warmth, and the love in their gaze, that empowers me. When it is over and I let go, I am instantly enervated. Hence, the need for bifocals.

Windows to the Soul

As I consider my own need for glasses, I am struck by my granddaughter's fascination with eyes. Perhaps her interest is true of all infants. Her favorite toys are the ones with eyes. She has rings she prefers to chew on, and balls she prefers to squeeze, but it is the toys with eyes that get the warm hugs and kisses. With people, she will look deeply into their eyes, maintaining contact far longer than most adults can manage. If I cover my eyes, she turns away, as if I had somehow left the room and was no longer available to her.

If the eyes are truly the windows of the soul, perhaps infants know something the rest of us have long since forgotten. If my granddaughter could speak, perhaps she could explain to me the power I find in the eyes of the people who listen to me so lovingly and openly.

Grandparent God, open my eyes that I might see.

Lullaby Time

We rock in the big blue rocking chair, her blue-gray eyes staring deeply into mine, as I sing the lullabies my mother once sang, ancient mother-prayers steeped in earth wisdom. Holding my gaze, she begins to sing, a wordless harmony, matching my silences with her own rests, my melodies with her own variations. Song after song, she gently gives voice to the love that holds us both captive, until the little eyes droop in sleep.

Do you sing to me, Grandparent God, accepting the wordless prayers I try to voice, the melody I have yet to master, with the same enchanted love that has taken possession of my soul?

Stargazing

Who said that every wish would be
heard and answered,
When wished on a morning star . . . ?
What's so amazing that keeps us star
gazing . . . ?
                    The Rainbow Connection

We rose before dawn on a cold March morning to watch the comet Hale-Bopp make its appearance in the early spring sky of 1997. Hale-Bopp's last trip to our solar system happened when the druids were assembling Stonehenge and the Egyptians were building the pyramids. Two-hundred-thirty generations of our children will pass before a descendent of ours will see this comet again.

We Chestos are a family of stargazers. I know very little astronomy, but I have come to recognize the seasonal patterns of our own particular piece of New England sky. I'm star struck by the fact that the light from some of the stars we see has spent a hundred-thousand years traveling across the galaxy to our backyard. I'm star struck in knowing that some of those stars actually burned out thousands of years before we see them.

I have always wanted to believe that our own particular "light" is like starlight, that it could travel on beyond us, long after we have experienced the "burn out." The light we *were* would remain shining in another's night, offering a place of reference in a sky that could be eons and light years away.

It is time to introduce my granddaughter to the night sky. As I gaze into her eyes, it is no longer difficult to believe that my own light will shine long after the source has been extinguished.

Grandparent God, are we becoming eternal?

Natural
Disasters

We were on our way to a wedding when the electrical storm hit. Lightning streaked across the sky almost simultaneously with the thunder that rocked the car. Liz pronounced calmly from the back seat, "If I were a natural disaster, I think I would be a thunderstorm, all loud and flashy, stormy and windy, and suddenly, burnt out and sunny."

We laughed. It is the essence of her personality.

So if I were a natural disaster, what would I be? We bantered the question around, each of us discovering a reality the other three in the car could readily affirm.

I would be a hurricane. Any thought, emotion, new idea, even frustration, begins small in me, swirling around my inner self, the eye of quiet that is my center. It gathers force from the surroundings, the ocean beneath, until it becomes huge and swirling and traveling at unpredictable speeds. Then it collides with the land of other people's ideas, thoughts, and frustrations. It can be amazingly destructive before it heads quickly back to sea to be reborn over the water. I am definitely a hurricane.

My husband is an earthquake. The things that move him deeply happen hidden inside, shifting, cracking, until the surface breaks. Becky is a flood, holding back the frustration and anger until the dam finally breaks, then taking a long time for the waters to recede.

I have known blizzards, avalanches, tornadoes, monsoons, and landslides. I have worked with quicksand and chinooks, ice storms and tsunamis. Are we born with these tumultuous characteristics, or are they reflections of the personal earth we inhabit? Do they represent our weaknesses, or could they be the source of our greatest strength?

Made of Stardust

As I watch my granddaughter sleeping, I wonder what hovers beneath the surface. It is too soon to tell, little one, if you are hurricane or thunderstorm, earthquake or tsunami. I cannot protect you from the turmoil that may one day rage both outside and in. But if you let me, perhaps I can help you to discover the power that lies hidden in the fury.

Grandparent God, you knit me together in my mother's womb. Teach me to find the strength you have buried in the violence, to harness the wind and use it as gift.

The Voice
of the Shepherd

The setting was picture perfect. The back wall of the tiny church was one massive window, looking out on the snow-heavy trees lining Seneca Lake. A sound system was almost unnecessary for the eighty or so people who crowded the benches in the tiny building. The warmth of the space, the gentle chatter of the people, all helped to create the assurance that this would be a great retreat.

The murmuring silence was abruptly shattered with the screams of the two-year-old sitting on the bench behind me. Her father, the lector for the day, had just left her with her mother so that he could join the entrance procession. Her screams drowned out the miniature organ and the voices of the community throughout the entrance song. Wisely, the dad positioned the book quickly and left the sanctuary to sit beside her. Quiet fell as the celebrant began the reconciliation rite.

Engrossed in a book her mother was showing her, the little one failed to notice her father slip out of the pew for the first reading. But as soon as his voice filled the church, she resumed screaming. When the dad stopped reading, the little one was distracted again and quieted down, but the second reading proved even worse than the first. She knew her father's voice, and she knew he was not where she wanted him to be. The minuscule setting held no corner where the mother, melting with embarrassment, could take the child out of hearing range. I looked at my three pages of reflections and wondered how the community and I would fare.

As I stood up to give my reflection, the dad was trying to comfort and quiet his daughter's sobs. I glanced down at the text I was using. "The sheep know, and respond, to the shepherd's voice . . ." I read the line with a tentative smile and the community dissolved into laughter. I didn't need to say a thing.

The Shepherd's Voice

Katie was sitting in the bouncer, deeply engrossed in the dangling toys, grasping and pulling herself upward, trying desperately to stand in the little chair. Her concentration was so intense, she did not hear her father enter behind her.

He sighed wearily and began to unburden the tale of a long and frustrating day. Oblivious to the discouraged tone, impervious to the fact that the words were not even addressed to her, Katie dissolved into giggles and began to squirm around in her seat to find the source of that wonderful voice she knows and loves so well. No day, no matter how terrible, is equal to the power of that smile. Steve was on the floor in seconds. "Hi, Honey."

Grandparent God, does my response to your voice bring you joy when your world goes amok?

Sunrise

I'll tell you how the sun rose,
a ribbon at a time.

Emily Dickinson

There is a strange clock at work in my body when I am on retreat. It wakes me, long before dawn, and I am compelled to move outside while darkness still makes the rocks treacherous and the ocean black.

Bundled against the morning chill, I wait. The first bird begins singing long before there is any sign of light, somehow promising the light will come. Soon the air is filled with the cacophony of early bird song. Almost as if it has been shattered by the noise, the darkness begins to melt. Slowly, the night's spectral forms take shape in the gray, colorless light, like a black-and-white movie, slowly focusing on the screen, as an old light bulb gains strength.

There is a stillness, despite the birds: a stillness of the wind, a quietness to the ocean's waves, a kind of breathless waiting.

Orange streaks, the first sign of color in this black-and-white world, begin to appear where the ocean meets the sky. The horizon becomes more definite as the pink and purple stretch upward, painting the bottom edges of the Atlantic's ever-present morning clouds. The sky becomes a breathtaking riot of color and even the birds quiet down to watch.

The sun peeks over the edge of the world, and the first path of light, a narrow trickle of diamonds, begins stretching across the water toward me. It does not matter where I choose to wait for the moment, the sun always finds me, sending its rays directly toward my quiet sanctuary.

Color seeps back into the world so slowly, its presence is almost imperceptible. In a moment, the world has forgotten its color blindness. In an hour, it will take for granted the colors of the day.

Beauty of Dawn

As I sit on the floor playing with my granddaughter, my heart recognizes "sunrise." I am acutely aware of the almost moment-by-moment changes, the new color emerging with such spectacular beauty, the new sounds defining this little person. And suddenly, I am afraid, afraid I might forget the beauty of dawn in the full light of day.

Grandparent God, am I always sunrise in your eyes?

Katie's Nap

I sit quietly on the piano bench, watching my granddaughter awaken from her nap. Her eyes slide open just enough to reveal a tiny slice of gray blue sky. Miniature fingers flex gently as rapid eye movements begin to be visible beneath her translucent eyelids. Her little legs, deeply creased with baby fat, give a couple of involuntary movements, but still the eyes remain partially closed.

Do you sit by my side, Grandparent God, waiting, as I wander in and out of my own dreams, oblivious to your presence? Do you watch me sleep with the same enchanted love that makes my own heart burst and brings tears to my eyes? Have I ever acquired the gentle, graceful movement toward prayer that this little one has toward wakefulness?

Her eyes drift open completely, and she lies still as she takes in her surroundings, her eyes wandering from the far corners of the room, across the walls in slow and gentle absorption.

Soon her visual journey brings her to me, as I sit waiting, and her entire face explodes in smiles. Her little arms, not quite ready for focused movement, dance a wild invitation to be picked up, as her feet and legs join in her chaotic rhythm. You can almost hear her thinking, "I found you, Grandma!" Yes, indeed, little one, you found me, but did you know that I was there all along?

Grandparent God, do you sit by my side in the darkness of sleep, waiting for me to awaken and turn to you? O God, to welcome the awareness of your presence with such joyful abandon and trust! Grandparent God, delight in me, love me, let me move your heart and change your world as this child has changed mine.

Salt
of the
Earth

"I'll never forget the day I discovered the goodness of salt!"

My daughter made the comment as we worked together to prepare a meal. I laughed in recognition of her observation.

I had grown up in a family riddled with heart disease, high blood pressure, and premature death from heart attacks. Salt, at that time, was seen as much more of a culprit before we all turned our attention to cholesterol. In our home, salt was anathema. The only time it ever appeared on the table was when we had corn on the cob. My mother never used it in cooking and consequently, neither did I. Growing up, I thought of it as a particularly bad thing, and never understood why we spoke of virtuous people as "salt of the earth." I learned to avoid the expression as carefully as I avoided the source.

Years later, I agreed to do a parish retreat in upstate New York before I realized, much to my dismay, that the gospel for the opening Sunday was the salt of the earth passage from the Sermon on the Mount. It was definitely before I had "discovered the goodness of salt." I sat with a shaker before me on the dining room table, tentatively tasting. Salt does not taste particularly good on its own. Its only purpose is to bring out the natural flavor already present in the food being salted. It isn't the salt itself that is good, it is the food enhanced by its presence.

The people who are truly salt of the earth are not the ones we admire for their virtue and holiness. They are the ones who bring out the virtue and holiness in us, and in everyone whose lives they touch. To be salt of the earth is not about being a pillar of the community as much as it is about bringing out the goodness in others.

I finally understood, but my heart had not caught up with my head. The first reflection of the retreat was scheduled for the 7 a.m. Sunday liturgy and consequently, I was the first person to show up in the hotel lobby. The continental breakfast was beautiful, but the room was freezing. The young waitress stood clutching her arms about her, trying to roll herself into a ball or simply dissolve into her short-sleeved uniform.

The perpetual mother in me asked where her sweater was. She did not have one. I offered to go back to my room and get one that she could wear. She shook her head, looking even more miserable as I started my breakfast.

An elderly woman walked into the lobby. "Did you set all this up?" she asked the young waitress, her tone filled with admiration. I watched the young woman grow physically taller under the gaze of this guest. "Yes, I did."

"This is wonderful! You must be very good at what you do!"

The waitress smiled. She dropped her arms and raised her head, the cold suddenly forgotten.

I felt humbled in the presence of a woman who truly knew how to be salt for the earth.

Powerless to Resist

Katherine Emily, you are the salt of my earth. With you, I am more than I ever hoped or dreamed I could be. You bring out all that is gentle and good and selfless and I am powerless to resist your "seasoning."

Grandparent God, thank you for teaching me that a little salt goes a long way.

Crocuses

The crocuses have broken through the hard crust of winter that lines the lawn, creating brilliant splotches of purple and pink in a vast sea of March browns. We stop on our daily walk, and I lift my granddaughter from the stroller to the ground for a closer look. She is captivated by the colors, and as she giggles with delight, it suddenly occurs to me that she has never known spring. Her four months with us have been marked by barren yards, naked tree limbs, biting cold, and shades of brown. She has no way of knowing about the life hidden within the bleakness, no expectations of warmth, no memory of these small, colorful harbingers of spring.

To have hope, I suspect we need some experience of what it is we hope for. Once we have experienced that hope, it becomes impossible to deny the knowledge of the new life hidden in the visible death that envelops us.

Come, Katie, meet the crocuses, and let me teach you how to dream about spring.

Grandparent God, send crocuses into my dreary landscapes and teach me to hope.

The Swing

How do you like to go up in a swing,
 Up in the air so blue?
Oh, I do think it the pleasantest thing
 Ever a child can do!

The words are from a favorite poem in Robert Louis Stevenson's *A Child's Garden of Verses*. My mother taught them to me, riding on a large wooden bench swing in a public park near our home. I was four at the time, and I absorbed, like a thirsty sponge, anything that rhymed. My love for swings has as much to do with the poem and my mother as it does with the soothing rhythm and cool breezes that are so much a part of swinging.

What is it about a swing that satisfies such deep desires in us? We work hard at getting nowhere, but the sheer joy of the ride is enough. Like so much of life, the very force against which we work is the force that provides the ride.

One, Two, Three

Every child should have a swing. We hung one for Katie. She was vaguely interested, as I put her in and buckled the safety strap. I stood in front of her, pulled the swing toward me only slightly, and let it go. Her face filled with alarm that turned instantly to terror as she sensed I was not holding her. In that split second, her eyes sought mine for reassurance, then her expression melted into joy as the small arc brought her back to me. The second time she swung gently away, her look was more tentative, less alarmed, and she giggled as she came back. By the third swing, she was waving her arms and legs delightedly, confident in the little arc that would return her to my arms.

We have started counting, "one, two, three" as I hold her and let go. At "two," her face fills with anticipation. She knows what is coming. At "three," she squeals with delight, even before I let go. After several days of swinging, the swing has become her favorite place, and she is vociferous with her annoyance and displeasure when the weather, the insects, or just the telephone make it necessary to lift her out.

Grandparent God, when it feels like you have let go, keep my eyes on you. Help me to trust the forces that carry me back, the loving grandparent who only wants me to know the joy and freedom of the ride, and the homecoming that is part of each arc.

K-K-K-Katie

K-K-K Katy, beautiful Katy,
You're the only g-g-g-girl that I adore;
When the m-m-m-moon shines,
over the c-c-c-cowshed,
I'll be waiting at the k-k-k-kitchen door.
                Geoffrey O'Hara, *K-K-K-Katy*

It's an old war song that my grandfather, the only person who called me Kate, sang to me as a little girl. Now I am singing it to my granddaughter. From the time she was six weeks old, I would greet her with the song, clapping her tiny hands to the rhythm, waving them over her head for the "moon shine." At the end of the song, I would clap wildly and say, "yea, Katie!"

Then I would whisper softly, "It's your Gram, Love," as I kissed her. When my work took me on the road for too long a stretch, I would telephone to sing to her.

She first began smiling at the sound of her name, the one familiar word in her universe. The smile soon became a giggle as I waved her little arms over her head. Now, when I begin to sing, the smile of recognition is not just for her own name, but for me. It is her Grandma who sings, and it is not just her name, but the love with which it is sung, that creates the happiness in her face and the sunshine in her eyes.

Grandparent God, you have called me by name and I am yours.

"UP!"

The gesture came as Katie tired of playing on the floor with her toys. She cannot quite make it to a sitting position on her own, and rolling over had grown frustrating. As I leaned over the blanket to speak to her, she surprised me, raising both her arms up directly toward me, lifting her head, and cooing, almost growling, as forcefully as she could manage. "Up?" I questioned. The legs danced and then became rigid as she tried to lift herself by sheer force of will.

Real communication! I swooped her up off the floor and held her closely, making sure she knew someone was listening to these new words. She nuzzled deep into my neck, planting wet, open-mouth kisses on my chest and face, letting me know I had indeed gotten the message right.

If prayer is lifting the mind and heart to God, then I suspect God is doing the lifting.

Grandparent God, up!

Do You Like Butter?

May brought a week of unseasonable heat to our quiet New England town. Discouraged by the late April snow and startled by the May heat wave, flowers that normally stretch out their arrivals from mid-April to June all made a simultaneous, riotous appearance.

I sat with my granddaughter in the patch of "weeds" I let grow wild in the middle of our front yard. It was alive with forget-me-nots, violets, daisies and hundreds of buttercups. The honeybees ignored our presence as they carried on their own visitation with the blossoms around us.

There is an ancient rite of childhood connected with buttercups. I reach for a blossom, hold it under the baby's chin, and ask "Do you like butter?" Throughout my growing up years, we tested one another with the buttercups. If you liked butter, the yellow flower would be reflected under your chin. If you didn't like butter, no telltale yellow glow would shimmer on your skin. At least we were convinced this was so.

There is a wisdom hidden in the game, like so many childhood games. You must love the beauty around you for it to be reflected in your skin. Only by loving what the little golden bloom stood for could we expect to find the same beauty in ourselves.

It has been said that beauty is only skin deep. But where else would it be except in our skin, the only part of us visible to the rest of the world? Our skin reflects whatever love exists deep in our hearts. It is important to hand on to our children the sacred ritual. It is important to pick buttercups and hold ourselves responsible for reflecting the beauty of creation.

Grandparent God, are you holding a buttercup under my chin?

Bubbles

Today we discovered bubbles. As I breathed life into the transparent soap film, my granddaughter's eyes grew wide with wonder. The Philadelphia Philharmonic filled the backyard with Beethoven, while the family of house finch that had nested on the outside speaker added their voices. It was a fitting accompaniment to my granddaughter's laughter, a suitable symphony to give voice to the amazement on her little face. A fickle breeze carried the bubbles back to us as she bounced delightedly on my lap, gurgling and reaching for the rainbows that floated by her face. Each time she caught one, she pulled back in surprise at the unexpected disappearance of the fragile ball and the sudden wetness on her hand. Each time, she would reach for the wand, pushing it into her mouth in an attempt to imitate me, making it almost impossible to make any bubbles at all.

Grandparent God, give me the patience to delight in the rainbows and trust you to provide the breath.

Praise

I grew up during the charismatic renewal of the late 1960s. Suddenly, the rote prayers of petition and thanksgiving that had shaped my childhood were no longer enough. God did not need our thanks. God knew our needs. God wanted us to offer praise.

Everything was about praise. Song books were named *Glory and Praise* and *Songs of Praise*. People held "praise meetings," and there was even a television show, *Praise the Lord Club*. It was a time of spiritual exuberance, and while it certainly shaped my journey, I am learning it was far from the only, or even the best, way to pray.

One Thing To Offer

My granddaughter snuggles in my lap, laughing into my eyes. She recognizes me now. She knows my voice, my eyes, the funny songs I sing to her. She left her toys to scramble onto my lap and cuddle for a few minutes before returning to the serious business of "Rock-em, Stack-em." She has only one thing to offer me: love. It is more than enough. I stop everything and enjoy.

Maybe prayer is about much more than praising, or even thanking, or asking. I have always known that it was about something more than me, but perhaps it is also about something more than God. Perhaps it is about relationship, about choosing to sit quietly in recognition and love.

Grandparent God, hold me.

Yea!!

When do we learn to stop cheering for ourselves, to stop delighting in our own accomplishments? Who teaches us that celebrating ourselves is a form of pride and why?

Katie spoke her first real word today. I was swinging her in my arms when she dropped her toy on the floor. I lowered her body and she reached down and grasped it firmly.

"Yea, Katie!" I shouted, with real enthusiasm.

She giggled delightedly and threw the toy on the floor again. We repeated the entire process. By the time the toy had made its fifth trip to the floor, Katie chimed in, cheering for herself. "Yea!" she said clearly.

I called excitedly to my daughter in the other room as I put Katie down on the floor. To my amazement she sat up by herself and held her balance. Coming from the bedroom, my daughter was delighted to see the baby holding herself so well, thinking that was what I had called her to see.

"Yea, Katie!" said her Mom, clapping her hands.

Giggling delightedly, Katie clapped her hands and echoed, "Yea!"

I am in awe of the fact that this baby's first word could be one of such joyful self celebration!

Grandparent God, do you cheer with me, as I do with my grandchild, delighted in the joy of my own discovery?

Object Permanence

Peek-a-boo, I see you.

There is a particular stage of development in which babies acquire object permanence. For the first seven months, we can take something away, and as long as it is replaced by something else, it is instantly forgotten. As new parents, we somehow knew this instinctively, replacing inappropriate toys that found their way into our baby's mouth with teething rings or wet face cloths.

But, at some given point, the baby develops object permanence. She begins to look in the direction of the missing object, waiting, hoping it will reappear. This is the stage when "peek-a-boo" actually becomes fun and fosters this natural development.

Katie is developing object permanence. Her Mom is trying to nurse her on the couch, but she keeps pulling from the breast to make eye contact with me, checking to make sure I am still there. I try sitting on the other side of my daughter, and the baby cranes her neck to find me. Guilty over frustrating my daughter's efforts to feed her, I disappear into the kitchen and peek around the corner. Katie pushing away from the breast, following the direction of my departure, catches me peeking and giggles delightedly.

In my house, it has become a game. I disappear around the corner of the fireplace, and the living room grows silent. If I come back in the way I came, her eyes will greet me as her face breaks into a welcoming smile. If I slip in quietly from the other side of the room, it is possible to stand and watch her sitting absolutely still, alertly gazing at the place where I disappeared. My heart is touched knowing she is holding intact the memory of my presence, quietly waiting until I reappear.

> *Grandparent God, do you hide briefly so that we will learn to remember your presence? Do you watch to see if we are watching, delighting in our silent expectation?*

Fear

We are not born with fear. We are born with reflexes that react to loud noises and the sensation of falling, but not with fear. We learn fear. And at some point, we learn to be afraid of the things that could hurt us, things that startle us, things we don't understand.

As we grow old enough to recognize our fear, we begin to feel ashamed. So much of the sacred books of the world's great religions are filled with the command not to be afraid that we believe it must be something over which we should have at least some elemental control. When the control fails, we add guilt to our shame for our inability to trust.

Be not Afraid

Becky unintentionally frightened the baby. She had been holding Katie in her arms when she began to rinse the wading pool with the hose. The loud noise of the water on the plastic surface, and the spray that came back at them, startled the baby. Becky called in tears to tell me Katie would no longer go anywhere near the pool she had loved only the day before.

The following day, Ed sat on our deck, patiently playing with a small toy in our own replica of the wading pool. Several yards away, Katie watched warily from the shelter of my arms. As her grandfather grew more excited, she became more engrossed, eventually reaching tentatively toward him.

We waited several more minutes before I brought her a few steps closer. She clung for a moment, then turned her attention back to the pool. Gradually, a few steps at a time, we approached. It took almost an hour before she reached the edge of the water and placed her hands carefully in it. It was another half-hour before she could be persuaded to get in.

Grandparent God, as I gently enter the pool with my granddaughter, I finally understand you never meant "Fear not" to castigate me for my timidity. You simply meant I did not have to be afraid because you would always be with me. You would not push me into things beyond my limited courage. You would wait patiently by the side of the pool, holding me in your arms, gently enticing me, until I was ready to go in.

Forward Motion

Katie is learning to crawl. It is part crawl, part lunge. We put the toys slightly beyond her grasp, and she makes her way awkwardly across the floor to them. We sit and watch with the same rapt attention we would give to *Swan Lake*.

I stopped in at my daughter's home with a basket of flowers to celebrate her first day at her new job. Steve was feeding the baby on the couch. I tried to enter unobtrusively, sitting quietly at the far end of the couch, in the hope of not disturbing the baby, but Katie had caught sight of me. She pushed the bottle away, struggled from sitting to crawling, awkwardly moved along the couch, then lunged for my lap. I had seen her propel herself before as she struggled to reach her toys, the dog or the cat. But this time, it was to reach me!

In that incredible moment, I felt *chosen*.

Grandparent God, I choose you. As floundering as my efforts may be, I choose you.

The Sky
Is Falling

Fall has come with a radiant blaze of color. The air has the dry, crisp smell of hay and fallen leaves, pointing to the approach of winter. The surfaces of road and lawn have grown crunchy beneath my feet. The sky has settled into its deep autumn blue while the maples create brilliant designs on its cerulean canvas. Apples weigh down the orchards, and the house is alive with the deep cinnamon smell of pies baking in the oven. I am an October baby, and fall has always been my favorite time of year.

My granddaughter is not so sure. As I introduce her to a backyard suddenly painted in fresh new colors, she looks at me quizzically. Where is the deep familiar green canvas of summer? The nuts from the hickory attack us, and I catch them as they fall. Red maple and golden birch leaves drift to the ground. Katie is delighted by the color, but she gives the sky a wary, tentative look.

Only rain is supposed to fall out of that sky, soft summer rain that soaks her face and rattles on the umbrellas and skylights. Suddenly, colorful shapes and small hard spheres are falling from her sky. The canopy that has covered the backyard is slowly disappearing. The air is not cold enough yet for her to sense the difference, but soon, even the air she breathes will have lost its familiarity.

How can I comfort you, little one? How can I tell you that death is temporary, that resurrection comes every spring? You have not known enough of death to know the life that rests beyond. Let's rake the leaves and jump in them, make scrunching sounds with hands and feet, and rejoice in the moment, even when it is a dying that makes our fun possible.

The sky is not falling, Love. And even if it were, I would still be here to hold you safe. I will wait for the new life for you.

Grandparent God, do you offer me brilliant colors in the midst of the dying, crunchy promises of resurrection? Help me to trust you that spring will come again, even if I have not known enough of death to trust the dying.

Office Work

We have baby-proofed my office. From two-and-a-half feet up, it looks like a normal office, complete with fax and computer, bookshelves and cupboards. The lower section looks like a nursery, with blocks and toys, stuffed animals and small books, with pictures.

I work as Katie plays happily. She is an easy baby, able to amuse herself. Caring for her is not terribly demanding. I write, make phone calls, all the time chatting with her. Frequently she will become so absorbed in her play, she will forget that I am there. I suspect, in these moments, my stream of conversation becomes a kind of white noise—elevator music, unobtrusive.

And then, she draws herself up, holding onto my knees, and demands my undivided attention. We will do a story, or a song, or share a snack. She returns contentedly to her play. Such a wonderful, gentle rhythm she gives to our time together!

Grandparent God, do you set me down in a world you have prepared for me, watching and conversing gently, waiting for me to turn to you, demanding the attention that was always mine?

Soccer Prayer

The fall soccer season has started. Every town park is filled with tykes in brightly colored uniforms. The little ones running down the field like a small swarm of bees bring back memories of our own children's soccer days.

Liz was seven. She ended our grace before supper by asking God to help her score a goal in the evening's game. Her brother, older and wiser by five years, explained that she was not supposed to pray to score a goal. God couldn't really do that. She should pray to do her best.

"Well," she responded quickly, "If I did my best, I would score a goal."

I look at my granddaughter, playing happily with a miniature Winnie the Pooh soccer ball. What would I do if *you* asked *me* to help you score a goal? I couldn't come on the field and score it for you. Even if I wanted to, the referee wouldn't let me. That's not how the game is played.

I would practice with you, though. I would tell you everything I learned about the game from your grandpa who coached it and your own mother who played. I would even buy you cleats. And then I would stand on the side lines and cheer, whether or not you ever scored a goal!

Grandparent God, when it seems as if you are not hearing my prayers, am I the one who has failed to hear you standing on the sidelines cheering for me?

Baby Steps

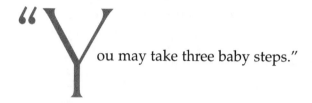

ou may take three baby steps."

"Mother, may I?"

"Mother, may I?" These words come from one of the revered games of my childhood. Because of my experience of this game, I grew up referring to tiny, hesitant steps, both physical and mental, as baby steps. There was always something slightly pejorative in the designation.

As I watch my granddaughter attempt to walk, I think of this understanding and question the wisdom of our labels. Katie is nine months old, pulling herself up on furniture, edging along things, and desperately wanting to walk. If you take her hands, she immediately steps, but not the "baby steps" of my childhood understanding. She lifts her foot so high, she could mount an eighteen-inch riser, then puts it down firmly, in the same spot where she started. Her efforts are not tiny, they are immense, even if they fail to propel her anywhere.

Maybe that was what we really meant by "baby steps," steps that did not get us anywhere, or at least not very far. Perhaps it is just another manifestation of our addiction to results. Our efforts are almost always measured in terms of what comes out of them. Watching this little baby step reminds me that what we put into them may be the most important factor of all.

Grandparent God, is it the effort and not the result that counts with you?

Well-Worn Stories

Marley was dead: to begin
with. . . . There is no doubt that Marley
was dead. This must be distinctly
understood, or nothing wonderful can
come of the story. . . .

A Christmas Carol

My mother's voice, and the funereal cadence she employed as she read those lines, echoes in my memory. Every December evening, for the first five years of my life, our entire family gathered around the stove in the kitchen as my mother read *A Christmas Carol* aloud, complete with her own special cast of voices. The tradition died when we moved away from my grandparents, but more than fifty years later, I can still recite whole sections of the first chapter, mimicking the rhythms my mother ingrained in me.

My own children grew up loving *Goodnight Moon*. Occasionally at a family gathering, they will begin reciting, exactly as it was once read to them. They will pause and drop their voices in unison just before the old lady whispers, "Hush!" then dissolve into laughter at the warmth of the shared memory.

Story Break

Katie has a favorite storybook, *Hand, Hand, Fingers, Thumb*. Before every nap, she reaches for it; whenever I suggest a "story break," she pulls it out of her little book rack. I can always interest her in a second story, but this one has to be first. It is not just the story that she loves, it is the crazy, sing-song way in which I tell it. Now, as soon as she takes the book in her hands, long before I begin to read, her little head starts bobbing, and her whole body begins to dance to a rhythm she has learned on a far deeper level than words.

Grandparent God, bury your stories deep in my heart so that I dance to the rhythm even when you are silent.

A Prayer for the Right Suit

My youngest daughter and I are in the car, making our way to Bloomingdale's in New York City. In the past week, we have exhausted the malls of Connecticut in our search for a suit appropriate for a medical residency interview. "Making our way" is an apt expression, since we have missed two turns, run into major construction, detours, and road blocks, and finally found ourselves on a street that has just put in restricted turns. We look longingly down the avenue we need, sadly acknowledge the new sign that prohibits turning onto it, and continue west four long blocks, beginning our second tour around the city!

Liz has put in several long weeks of study for the second level of her medical licensing exam. She is both tired and disgusted with herself over the simple navigational problem. I try to comfort her, saying, "Never mind. It is giving me that much more time to pray that you will find the suit you need."

"Mom, I thought you're not supposed to pray for things like that!" This from the child who once prayed to score a soccer goal!

"Of course I can pray for things like that. I know that God isn't going to put a suit in Bloomingdale's for you, but I can pray that our eyes will be open to see the suits that are there and to find one that will fit and be appropriate."

We found the suit in the first ten minutes of shopping.

No Such Reservations

Katie has no such reservations about reaching for anything she wants. I don't want that to change when she has the words to ask. I want my granddaughter to believe she can ask me for anything, whether or not it is something I can do or give. I want her to trust me enough to let me explain my answer.

> Grandparent God, teach me to ask simply, like a well-loved grandchild, for all that I need. Preserve me from theologically correct prayer and spiritually astute intercessions.

87

Standing

Katie stood by herself for twenty long seconds. She had pulled herself up along the magazine rack that holds her books in the special corner we reserve for reading. She kept one hand lightly in place as her little body sought its center of balance. Her free hand reached for one of the new books we had placed in the rack. As she pulled it out, both hands were needed to open it and her other hand moved easily off the edge of the rack. She balanced, "reading" her book, distracted into doing what she does not yet realize she can do.

Grandparent God, you gently invite me to trust myself, distracting me into risking, placing far more faith in me than I have in my own balance or ability.

Called Home

I grew up in an age when parents stood on their back steps and called their children's names when they wanted them to come home. My mother's strong, husky voice would linger on the evening quiet, and I would know play was just about over. But I would still try to delay the inevitable.

It was never acceptable to shout back, "What?" A far better delay tactic was to shout, "Yes?" which was a less obnoxious way of saying the same thing. The message would come ringing back, a little more imperiously. "Supper."

There was only one acceptable response to that command. "Coming, Mom." My mother much preferred *that* to be the first response, but most nights we could get away with "Yes." "What?" could bring an end to the playing privileges of the following day. Looking back, I can't imagine what we were thinking. My mother would not have been standing outside calling my name if she did not need me to come home, no matter what the reason.

Called and Loved

What does it mean to be called? What does it mean as I call your name, Katherine Emily, and turn your attention to me? I would not interrupt you for superficial reasons. I want you to know, you are called because you are loved. The one who calls has good things in store for you.

Grandparent God, teach me to say "Coming."

Fire

Some say the world will end in fire,
Some say in ice. . . .
I hold with those who favor fire.
Robert Frost

Flames wrap themselves like arms around the kindling in our wide, open hearth. Slowly gathering strength, they carefully pick at the bigger logs. Soon, yellow, blue and orange streaks begin a hypnotic dance as the crackling sets its own cadence.

The air warms first, taking the edge off the early morning chill. By afternoon, the stones will be radiating their heat. By the time the sun stops streaming through our southern windows, we will scarcely notice the winter drop in temperature.

The fireplace, for me, has always been the most important possession in our home, except, perhaps, the piano. Countless minor tragedies and a few major ones have been made bearable by a soothing cup of tea in front of the open fire. Fire evokes a profound emotional response in me: I struggle to identify an anonymous echo of some ancient ancestor who found in the flames something we have collectively forgotten.

Reverence

This is Katie's first fire. She stands mesmerized, eyes glued to the flame, body intent and still. Minutes pass. Then slowly, tentatively, she approaches, registering the change in temperature with a slightly puzzled look. It is time for the warnings about fire, about the danger of getting burned. So I gather her in my arms as we both sit on the floor before the hearth. We hold our hands out to the heat and I gently warn, "Hot. Don't touch." But she is not really interested in touching. She returns to the stillness, gaze intent on the flames. I begin to sing softly to her; it feels like an appropriate accompaniment to the moment. As I look down at her almost passionate concentration, I see my own, unnamed feeling mirrored in her face. And suddenly I know—it is reverence.

Katie, let me tell you about our awesome God.

Grandparent God, I think I have discovered your fingerprints on my soul.

The Mall

I hate shopping, especially in malls. The crowds, the rushing, the tremendous array of "stuff" all make me feel overwhelmed and a little claustrophobic. By early November, the Christmas decorations add to the visual bombardment, and the shoppers all begin to look stressed and haggard, more like the exhausted business commuters I meet in airports than like the happy revelers they are supposed to be.

I took Katie to the mall to find a birthday present for her Mom, a late November baby. The stores were a little quieter—I had deliberately chosen a Monday morning for this expedition—but the few customers seemed even more intense and serious. There were no Saturday window shoppers to alleviate the level of serious business.

Katie looked at every person who passed, doing her best to distract them. Those who noticed and made eye contact were instantly rewarded with one of her "scrunchy" face smiles and a whole litany of the many noises she delights in making.

One person after another melted in her presence, stooped to her eye level, and engaged in a totally senseless conversation. After a few moments of delighting each other, some adults would straighten up, smile wordlessly at me, and continue on their way. Some would take a moment to ask her age, her name, our relationship.

She made no distinctions. People I might never have approached, or even seen, stopped to talk to her, and eventually, to talk to me. Katie's smiles, her words, her funny faces, were for everyone who took the time to notice. If they responded in any way, she reached out happily. I waited and watched quietly, letting her work her magic, feeling as if I had been given the opportunity to bestow a special blessing on the Danbury Fair Mall.

Katie, how does Christmas shopping sound?

Grandparent God, did you send us a baby because you knew we couldn't resist?

My
Mother's Voice

I am standing by the stove making soft custard for Thanksgiving dinner. As I stir, I hear my mother's voice:

"Keep the heat really low. Keep stirring. You don't want the custard to get too hot. It will curdle if it does."

I keep stirring, playing the tapes in my mind. My mother no longer remembers how to make custard. Like so many of the things that shaped my childhood, the recipe has been stolen by her Alzheimer's. My mother no longer knows about Thanksgiving, but her words live on in my mind.

"Even if it curdles, it will be okay. You can beat it with a whisk. It will be thin, but it will still taste good."

I have made soft custard every Thanksgiving for the last thirty-two years. Sometimes it curdles; sometimes it is too thin. But every year, my mother stands beside me, guiding my hands as she did when I was young. Her spirit is alive in the custard, the cookies, the mince tarts that were all so much a part of her holiday preparations. It is good, because her spirit is no longer with us in the body that lingers in the shadows of dementia.

Plant My Voice

I want to teach my grandchild to make soft custard. I want to tell her about stirring and keeping the heat low so that it won't curdle. But most of all, I want to plant my voice deep in her heart.

Grandparent God, teach me to listen over and over again to your word, so that it will not need to be spoken in order to echo in my heart.

The First Snowfall

It's winter, it's winter,
the snow fell last night,
It fell on the tree tops
and painted them white. . . .

I sang the words to my children with every first snowfall of the year. We would sit at the sliding glass doors to our deck and watch with wonder as the world was painted white. Then we would all bundle into our snowsuits and attack the hill in front of our house with sleds and "flying saucers." The red plastic disks worked best, needing no path for a sled's runners. By the time our frozen toes forced us inside, our cheeks were bright red, our noses runny, and our clothes soaked. We would strip down in front of the fire, put on warm clothes and share hot cocoa. My children continued sledding into their teen years and adult life, carrying with them happy memories of winter play.

I always loved the snow. As a child, winter vied mightily with fall as my favorite season, and winter sports were definitely my favorite childhood games. There is something so beautiful about the world covered with snow—like a benediction—temporarily releasing it from its winter barrenness. There is a quiet that comes with the snow, a silence that settles over the normal forest sounds, the restless children in a classroom, the noisy streets in a city. It is as if the world were saying "Shhh!"

Throughout my life, both as child and young mother, snow closures represented a sudden gift of time, a whole day not committed already to other tasks, an invitation to go outside and play. But time has taken a toll on my love of snow. Too many years of shoveling, too many cancelled jobs, too many times of being stranded far from home, have all started to wear the sheen off my winter wonder.

Bring Snowsuits

The Wednesday before Thanksgiving gave us Katie's first snowfall. (The only real snow of her unseasonably warm first winter had come on the day she was born.) I called my daughter to see if she had sung her the song, and was distressed to learn she did not remember the words. Never mind, we could sing it tomorrow. Bring snowsuits!

Thanksgiving Day dawned bitterly cold with a biting wind. Sledding would need to be postponed. But my granddaughter stands with her hands on the sliding glass doors, staring at the hemlocks and birches that are bending under their weight of snow, mesmerized by the sun sparkling off the icicles that hang from the eaves. As she stands awestruck before a frozen world, my own heart melts, stirring back to life a forgotten wonder reflected in her face.

I was taught in a thousand subtle ways, that God is found primarily inside churches. Looking at my granddaughter's entranced expression, it is difficult to understand how anyone could have convinced me this was true.

Grandparent God, Katie and I are going to take our sleds and go knock at your door. Can you come out and play?

Plum
Pudding

Every Christmas, we end our meal with plum pudding, a strange concoction made of figs and raisins and citron and suet, but no plums. We place the pudding in the middle of a large platter, douse it with liquor, then set it on fire. All the lights are turned off for the event, and we sing until the blue flame burns itself out.

The custom began with some ancient English ancestors, and I suspect the songs they sang were old English Carols. When my own English grandmother married an Irishman, they added a few Irish ballads. The young family eventually immigrated to South Boston, and "God bless America" was added to the carols and ballads, along with a little more whiskey to keep the flame burning. With the advent of the Second World War, "It's a Long Way to Tipperary" became part of the ritual, although why that particular song became their "war song" has never been quite clear to me. By the time my own children came along, the custom had extended to include Thanksgiving, and we had added "Feliz Navidad" for my sister's husband, who spoke no English.

The puddings were once made months in advance of the holidays and stored, wrapped in cheese cloth, in a crock in the pantry. The dregs of any stray liquor bottles were always added to the crock. We no longer make our pudding; we buy it in a can. After we sing and burn it quite black, we all eat the soft custard that is made to go over it. The pudding gets wrapped in foil and stored in the refrigerator. No one even likes it any more. A few weeks later, when it has grown moldy, it will be thrown out.

Growing up, my children all ridiculed the tradition. "Are we going to sing to the pudding again this year?" But as they reached college age, they started inviting friends home to share in the custom. Asked at one of our family education meetings what made us special and different as a family, my young adults all responded "We sing to plum pudding!"

It is not about dessert any more. As crazy as it sounds, it is about who we are as a family. Like every good ritual, it has matter (pudding) and form (lighting and singing). It connects us to our past and has expanded over the years to include the changes that came into our present.

This Thanksgiving, we introduced Katie to the plum pudding. She watched the blue flame, mesmerized, much too fascinated to join in the singing. Long after the lights came back on, she stared at the black lump in the middle of the table, as if something else wonderful could still come out of it now that the flame was gone.

Welcome to the family, Katherine Emily.

Grandparent God, are the rituals simply to remind me that I am yours?

The Joy
of the Ride

The cool, gentle breeze and the clear blue skies left no hint of the violent storm that had struck during the night. But the sea had not forgotten. The waves towered above the horizon, rushing violently toward the shore, only to crash and race backwards to the sea, dragging huge quantities of the beach along with them.

I navigated the shore carefully that morning, my two canes digging deeply into the wet sand. The bathers and sun worshipers from the day before had all disappeared. Only those who took the sea seriously were on the shore that morning. The surfers were out in force, many challenging the monster waves, skimming gracefully along the frothy edges.

As they danced an intricate ballet on the surface of the water, I envied them the lithe bodies that responded so gladly to their bidding. But my heart was most truly captured by the ones who could not quite master the difficult surf. After tumbling again and again into the rough waters, they settled for riding their boards belly down. It is not form that counts, after all, but the joy of the ride.

It was not a bad message for one whose own ride was often far from graceful.

The Skootch

That misty memory from an almost forgotten Virginia vacation was evoked this morning by my granddaughter's curious mode of locomotion. Katie has not quite mastered walking, but she has discovered that it is all about hands. Crawling gets you places, but it does not leave your hands free for anything else. Like the belly surfers of my reminiscence, Katie has devised a substitute. Kneeling with one knee on the floor and the other foot firmly planted in front of her, in a kind of genuflection, she has discovered she can propel herself by stepping forward while balancing herself with one hand on the floor. This leaves the other hand free for carrying. Her skootch is rapid, easily as effective as the belly surfing, and far more unique.

Katie's mother is eager for her to walk. "She can stand alone." "She is almost one." "It is time." I say nothing, but I am in no rush.

Skootch just a little longer, Katie, and remind me it is not the form but the joy of the ride that counts.

> Grandparent God, help me to treat my own limits with both the love I give this baby, and the delight I find in her inventive compensation.

First
Birthday

The cake, the presents, the balloons, the company that fills the living room, are all a little confusing. Katie is bewildered by the gifts and toys pressed upon her by well-meaning guests. As we sing "Happy Birthday," she looks warily around the room, as if we had all taken sudden leave of our senses.

Grandparent God, do I sometimes distrust you simply because your love is so lavish?

Christmas

The Christmas tree we cut down this year is only twelve feet tall. It is dense, with a perfect, somewhat narrow, Nutcracker Ballet shape, but definitely smaller than trees of the past. The manger scene has also shrunk, from the large village that once spread across the living room floor in our old home, to the middle shelf of the china closet. Still, there is no mistaking as you walk in our door, it is Christmas.

I love Christmas. The wonderful stories, the family rituals, the caroling, the decorations, the baking, the shopping (well, maybe not the shopping, but definitely the surprise and joy the gifts always seem to bring), all conspire to make it one of my favorite times of the year. When we looked for our first home, I would obligingly glance at the kitchen first (every real estate agent insists a woman is most interested in the kitchen!) and then I would get to the important issue: Was there a good place for the Christmas tree?

Christmas is the family's most important feast. The churches argue for Easter, but they will never win. The idea of a God who would come as a baby captures the hearts and imaginations in a way that redemption and resurrection never can. If the world outside the churches latched on to Christmas and turned it into a Madison Avenue frenzy, perhaps it is because of the instinct we possess for the divine found within each of us, a divinity that needs to be welcomed and celebrated.

It is Katie's first Christmas. She is fascinated by the sheer size of the tree that has invaded her grandparents' living room. She looks quizzically at us and gently touches the little lights, too cool to burn her fingers. We watch as she explores the unbreakable ornaments hung on the lower branches, just for her, her eyes wide with delight and awe.

The presents are a little overwhelming, but there is all that wonderful paper and ribbon. Opening a gift can be just as much fun as the gift itself, and even the wrappings can be treated with love.

Grandparent God, teach me to take the same delight in the process of discovering your gifts as I take in the gifts themselves. Teach me to look with wonder, even as I try to create wonder for others. And Grandparent God, Happy Birthday.

Wanting

We interrupted Katie's nap. We were going to be gone for a week, and I wanted to visit before we left, but we would not have intentionally awakened her.

She turned over and looked up as my daughter and I tiptoed into the room. Becky lifted her up, but she was not really awake.

And now she sits, snuggling against her mother's chest, thumb in her mouth, finger hooked over her nose, eyeing me warily.

"It's your Grandma, " my daughter reminds her gently.

I smile, but she will have none of it. She burrows her head more deeply into her Mom's breast.

As she awakens a little more and begins to smile at her Grandpa's antics, Becky suggests I take her.

"Let's wait. I am in no rush." I want her to *want* to come to me.

It only takes a few more minutes before she stretches out her arms, and I scoop her up lovingly.

Grandparent God, do you wait patiently for me to want you?

Walking

A ship in the harbor is safe, but that is not what ships were built for.

Katie is ready to walk. She is cruising around the furniture, one hand securing her balance as she quickly steps along. But she is limited to the pieces of furniture available. She can only travel where those pieces allow. Eyeing me warily as I sit on the hearth across the room, she recognizes she can only reach me if she is willing to let go.

How many times do I limit myself to the places where there is "furniture" to hold? How often do I go in circles because I am afraid to let go, afraid to risk falling? Have we constructed religions so that we might have furniture to hold on to, ways to convince ourselves we are walking on our own, even though the limits have been so clearly marked by another?

Katie travels around the table several more times, making her way to the end of the couch and stretching out her hand to me. I reach out my arms and realize I am holding my breath as she stands motionless, then comes careening across the small expanse of open floor. I swing her up in my arms, amazed at her wobbly grace and profound bravery.

Grandparent God, you who planted courage deep in our hearts, are you still awestruck as it emerges?

Gently

"**G**ently, gently!"

Katie has thrown herself on the dog and wrapped her arms lovingly around his neck. Even her twenty pounds can be rough on an old dog, too gentle himself to react in any way to her surprise attack. The cat is less amenable and swats a little, then looks at me for assistance. This is her house. She will not move for this intruder.

Since Katie has found her legs, she goes through the house like a whirlwind, unaware of the possible damage she could do to herself, to the other creatures in her wake, or the house itself. She reminds me of my own dash through life and how often I am oblivious to the effects of my own actions. The warning, "Gently, gently," is for myself, as much as it is for her.

When my daughter arrives at two-thirty, Katie is asleep in her crib and I am curled up exhausted in my big rocker. Becky glances around the room and says, "Looks like a baby has been here." I look around at the books Katie emptied from her little book rack, the toys and stuffed animals strewn across the floor, the little people from her animal train sitting on the piano, and the cat hiding up on a beam. We laugh together and once Katie awakens, we show her how to help us restore the order she has decimated.

Grandparent God, are you waiting for me to wake up, to pay attention to the effect of my presence on others, on myself, on my world? Help me, as I help Katie, to learn to walk gently on the earth, to leave nothing but footprints in my wake.

Piano Man

If you said goodbye to me tonight,
There would still be music left to write.
What else could I do? I'm so inspired
by you. . . .

> Billy Joel, *For the Longest Time*

I was driving home from a parish retreat in a little village five hours west of nowhere. Interstate 80 stretched silently in front of my early morning journey. Billy Joel was bellowing from my CD player, filling the lonely spaces with his greatest hits. There is something striking about a compilation of an artist's greatest hits. A new CD has a few songs that might actually make it, and a lot of others that won't. But a greatest hit album has all the best songs, the ones that have already proven themselves.

Listening to them strung together, it is sometimes possible to find some basic connection that is the underlying reason for their success and durability. The truth slowly dawned on me that all of Joel's greatest songs reflect some type of deep, personal experience. It is as if each of the moments had been too profound to be experienced all at once, something Joel almost attests to: "If you said goodbye to me tonight, there would still be music left to write. . . ."

As those words slowly melted into my consciousness, I began to understand Monet's water lilies, Eliot's *Wasteland*. They each represent a moment when life was too deep to be contained in the time in which it happened, and it simply overflowed. Those moments may be as profound as Beethoven's Ninth or as simple as my storytelling. Each is a moment that has not been fully absorbed and cries out to be recorded. There is a generosity in art that invites the other to enter into the depths of the artist's experience, but there is also a compulsion that makes it necessary to share. If the artist were to be silent, the very stones would shout.

Katie is playing piano with me. She sits on my lap and rests her hands on the keyboard as I make music. Sometimes, she will add her own harmony. Today she waits quietly until the rests, then punctuates it with her own music. Occasionally, she reaches up and removes the sheet of music in front of us and opens another book. Somewhere in those books are the different sounds that come from her Grandma's hands, and she wants to enter into the mystery. Her head bobs and her little body dances in my lap to the rhythm.

I watch quietly, charmed by her amazing sense of timing and her love for the music. At one time in my life, I would have already been planning the lessons; there would have been an urgency to develop the gift I sense in the little body rocking rhythmically in my lap. After all, I was taught that gifts came with responsibility: "to whom much has been given . . . ," "don't bury your talents," and all that.

As a grandparent, I can no longer believe in a God whose gifts come as burdens. I will teach this child to play, but not because she needs to use this talent wisely. This gift was given so that when her own life experience is too deep to be contained, she will have a way to express the overflow.

Grandparent God, teach me to accept my own gifts, no strings attached.

Powerlessness

Slowly, I am discovering how it is possible to believe in Divine Omnipotence and still know there are times when that Divine is powerless.

There are many things for which God is in no way responsible. I have probably known that for years, but there has always been that quiet little voice in the back of my head that said, "WHY not?" If you are all powerful, God, why not?

I disagreed with my daughter on a decision she and Steve made for the baby. It was such an insignificant thing that I forgot about it as soon as the conversation was over, but I remembered biting my tongue, conscious of my own powerlessness. I knew I could ignore my daughter's desires when her daughter is with me. I might have even had the power to convince her, if I had tried, that I had a better idea. After all, I have age and experience on my side. But it would have been at the risk of threatening her own beautifully blossoming sense of maternal authority.

This is *her* child, and I remained quiet, out of love for both of them.

Grandparent God, do you choose to be powerless, rather than rob us of our power?

God of Light

My husband owns a flashlight that is actually more like a spotlight or, perhaps, a headlight. It was a Christmas gift from his brother and it has become our companion on late evening walks. We have often tried aiming its wide beam at clouds or low-flying planes to explore its actual reach. Whether or not it can illuminate the clouds, however, is not as important as the simple fact that it lights our path.

There was a time in my life when it felt as if God walked ahead of me with just such a light. My only task was to keep close enough to follow, to stay in the light.

I still meet people who are gifted with this kind of light. It is hard not to envy their security, their absolute assurance that they know exactly what God wants of them. It is also hard not to be annoyed by their equal assurance they know exactly what God wants of me.

I am not sure when the wide-beamed light disappeared from my life. At some point, it had become a simple flashlight with a narrow beam, illuminating a small circle in front of me, as if God were walking beside me. My following had become "walking with"; a "walking with" in which I shared the decisions about direction.

But the circle of light became smaller, and I realized God had fallen behind me. Now the light was pooled around my feet. There was no indication of what lay ahead, no way to see into the darkness down the road. I no longer followed the light, or even walked with it. It was almost as if the light followed me, carefully lighting each step, showing what lay underfoot, but no more than that. The decisions had all become mine. I missed the wide-beamed flashlight, I missed the simple task of following. I even missed the shared decision making that had come with the narrow beam. But the light was still there.

Then darkness came.

It isn't as if I did anything to bring it on, it isn't as if I made some effort to step out of the light. The battery simply died. The light was gone, and it wasn't just darkness, but terrifying emptiness, that overwhelmed me in its absence.

In the Darkness

I was curled up in my usual prayer spot on the living room rocker. My youngest arrived home from her summer job with the usual noise and deposit of clutter that accompanied all her entrances. She dropped a kiss on my cheek as lightly as she dropped her shoes, her sweater and her purse, then she stopped and stared.

"What's wrong, Mom?" Until that moment, I had not realized my cheeks were wet with tears. I looked deeply into the gray hazel eyes filled with concern and compassion. How do you explain the darkness to a twenty-year-old college student who seems to walk through life under her own particular sunbeam?

"Mom? Let me make you a cup of tea." If there is any burden in life that cannot be made lighter by a cup of hot tea, my family has not found it.

As we sat, warmed as much by the comfortable love as the steaming liquid, I shared the journey I had made from light into darkness. I did not expect her to understand, only to listen.

The light was completely gone. I had been left in the dark.

She took my face in her hands, wiped away the tears that had come again with the telling, and looked in my eyes as she said, "That's because the light is within you now."

That's because the light is within you. Is that what the darkness means, not that we have been abandoned, but that we have absorbed and been absorbed?

Trusting the Light

Katie has inherited her grandparents' love of flashlights! The wide-beamed light of our evening walks is still too heavy for her, but she loves the small, pencil-shaped light her Grandpa keeps next to the bed. She is not yet able to manage the switch, but she knows the light is hidden inside. She will twist and turn it, "shining" it on surfaces and expecting the light to appear. Once it has been turned on for her, she will walk around the house with it, not reserving the beam for dark corners, but spending it lavishly on every surface. Even after the battery dies, she does not lose interest. She will sit quietly, carefully examining the silver pencil, convinced the light is simply hiding, waiting for it to reappear.

Grandparent God, help me to trust the light, even when it is hidden inside me.

To My
Granddaughter

I hold you in my arms, Katherine Emily, and quietly acknowledge you have changed my universe. Did you know that your birth came at a terrible time in our world? I saved the newspapers—*The New York Times, The Danbury News-Times*—with their front page pictures of the tragedy that rocked our world the autumn you were born.

Everyone told me it was silly to save papers that would deteriorate and yellow, papers that needed to be carefully stored. After all, the pictures and the stories would all be preserved in libraries, computers, books. But I need you to know, little one, that this happened to *us*. These are the papers that came into our home, the stories we read with our morning coffee. The smudges in the print are from our tears.

Something terrible happened, Katie, and many, many people died. Some died on the outside and some, like your Gram, died on the inside. Some stopped believing in God, because something terrible was done in the name of God. And some stopped believing that we mattered, that any one of us mattered at all. How could our minuscule efforts, our worn-out prayers, possibly count in the face of so much evil?

And then you were born. Tiny, helpless and beautiful, the most significant event in the whole troubled world, blissfully unaware of your power and your importance. And as the universe shifted to make room for you, I recognized we do not have to know we are significant for it to be true.

As I care for you, so God cares for me. As I believe in you, so God believes in me. As I love you, so God loves me.

Grandparent God, do I rock your universe?

Kathleen Chesto writes and lectures about spirituality and family life. Her articles have appeared in *National Catholic Reporter, U.S. Catholic* and *Liguorian*. Her most recent book is *Raising Kids Who Care* (Ligouri, 2003). She holds a doctor of ministry degree as well as a bachelor's degree in education and a master's degree in religious studies. She lives in Southbury, Connecticut.